In memory of my grandfather, Ted T. Turner,
a private artist who inspired me to go public.

FOREWORD*

If not for God, fear would have an undefeated record. If not for God, fear would have kept my dear friend TiffyTalks from embarking on her own personal journey that would lead to the birthing of this book!

The Bible tells us in 2 Timothy 1:7, "For God did not give us a spirit of timidity, but a spirit of power, of love and of self-discipline." In the pages that follow, Tiffany is challenging you, the reader, to take God at His word...not hers. You see, while she is the author, God is the inspiration and His call for you, right now, is to break free of fear and embrace the change that He's been calling you to for weeks, months, and maybe even years. Will responding to God's call be easy? Of course not, but thankfully, you have this book to help you. Not only will this book open your mind and heart to hear the voice of God in your life, but it will challenge you to be intentional in your approach to change through the various "Key to Consider" moments that await at the end of each chapter. So, if you're serious about obtaining the best life God has for you, the life you've allowed fear to keep you from, then this book is for you.

Enjoy and may God bless!

In Christ,

Armond Mosley
Author & Coach

NOTE TO READERS*

* {
This publication includes experiences, opinions, as well as ideas of the author. Although the author and publisher have made every effort to ensure that the information in this book was correct at press time, the author and publisher do not assume and hereby disclaim any liability to any party for any loss, damage, or disruption caused by errors or omissions, whether such errors or omissions result from negligence, accident, or any other cause.

The reader should consult a competent professional before applying or adopting any ideas in this book.

ACKNOWLEDGEMENTS*

*{ Special and continual thanks to my daughter, Deja, for challenging me to grow... to my family, friends, professors and blogger boos who allowed me to lean on them... and to the unknown people who prayed on my behalf, thank you!

Lastly, to all the women surveyed who allowed me to interrupt their lives for just a few minutes, and in some cases hours, to get to know them and what they care about better, I appreciate your honesty. And thanks, most of all, to God—who heard my cry for change and answered my call.

CONTENTS*

INTRODUCTION*

{

* In 2013 I set about interviewing dozens upon dozens of women between the ages of 24 and 45, from diverse cultures, faith backgrounds, and professions. I was part of a think tank for entrepreneurially minded women at the time, and it was the think tank leader who suggested it.

When I joined the think tank, I was already four years into a program of theological training and personal development, which had led me to experience an incredible physical and spiritual transformation. It was already very clear to me that I was meant to help and serve women through coaching, speaking, and writing, but just exactly how I was going to do this great work was still fuzzy. My leader suggested I do this interview-based survey of women in order to clarify my vocational purpose and better connect with those I wanted to help and serve.

To be perfectly honest, I was nervous about conducting the surveys. I wasn't sure how women, especially women I didn't know, would receive my request to dig into their deepest hopes and fears. My nervousness wasn't because I lack personal skills. I naturally have a knack with people, and my ability to relate to the pains of women is real. Like a lot of women I know, I understand what it's like to struggle to raise a child as a single mom or to be left brokenhearted because the relationship you thought would be "the one" didn't translate into more than experience gained and time lost. For lack of a better term, I would say I'm a "woman's woman."

However, despite the multiple ways in which I could relate with these unknown women, I was still a little "shook" by the task ahead and had no idea how the interviews would impact me, and my purpose. But I was open enough to try and find out, and thankfully my apprehensions didn't stop me.

The more interviews I did, the more I realized I had to dig deeper, and I needed to speak to more women to do it. I was texting friends of friends to see if they would be interested in being part of the survey. I also reached out to a few ladies at church and to other entrepreneurial women. Essentially I was open to interviewing any woman who was willing to help me better understand what today's woman cares about.

Well, my findings were life changing — and also life affirming!

I realized that regardless of age, culture, faith background, or profession, women in general care deeply about *being essential (Do I matter?), being in relationship (Am I loved?), and being engaged in purposeful work (Will I leave a mark?).*

When I listened to each woman's confident responses (or lack thereof), I was affirmed that I am not alone. As women, none of us are alone. We are not alone in our apprehensions, hopes, and fears. We are not alone in our struggle to want to have control, nor are we alone in our sincere desire to want to relinquish control to something or someone greater than ourselves.

In some instances, I heard determination, strength, and willingness to take risks. In other instances, I heard angst, frustration, and fear of the unknown. Essentially, I heard the tensions that come with life, and how major disappointments and denials can diminish even the strongest woman's confidence.

But isn't this just how life can be?

Many of us are in a habitual state of flux—between strong and weak, capable and incapable, sure and unsure. The mixed emotions of these women spoke to my heart and reminded me of myself on so many levels. I was inspired by their voices to reflect on my story, my trials and my triumphs. I also was able to appreciate how my life story divinely bumped up against their life stories.

Now I had to do the harder work of figuring out what dots God wanted me to connect. How would everything I've been through—the bumps, bruises, and blessings—be used to speak to the strains and the strengths of women today?

As time went on, long after the surveys had been conducted, I sat with the gift of all my findings, and I placed the beliefs, frustrations, and worries of the women I'd interviewed up against my life's journey and my theological training, and gave it all to God in hopes that I would give birth to an idea, a mission, a movement that would ultimately empower and serve women.

"*As we move from a skeptical, disempowered, and disengaged place in life to a more hopeful, empowered, and engaged place in life, our light is able to really shine.*"

~@tiffytalks

"For my thoughts are not your thoughts, neither are your ways my ways,' declares the LORD" ~Isaiah 55:8

Well, I'm thrilled to say, "God responded!" But it turned out that my thoughts were tiny in comparison to God's thoughts. I was thinking my vocational purpose would be safe, private, yet still impactful, but God was encouraging me to take risks, to go public, and to leave the impact all up to God. My theological studies, my personal and spiritual development had all conspired to lead me to this moment—the moment when I would step out and commit my life to helping others courageously embrace their unique purpose and spiritual power.

As a result, in February 2014, I launched *www.tiffytalks.com*, a multi-motivational platform, which includes purpose-driven coaching, motivational speaking, and inspirational blogging. The heart of TiffyTalks is to empower women (and girls) to #GetEngaged with their authentic value, voice, and vocation.

Through considerable reflection, research, and wrestling with my own spiritual journey, I have found five common obstacles that can block, (even blind) women from knowing their intrinsic value, forming healthy relationships, and aligning with their vocational purpose. I call this the **"I would love to, but"** list."

- **Would love to** make a change, but there's a fear of the unknown.
- **Would love to** be rid of someone or something that has her feeling stuck, but can't picture life without it or him/her.
- **Would love to** live according to her true value, but her sense of worthiness isn't clear or connected to how God sees her.
- **Would love to** not be so concerned about what people think, but still worries about likability and pleasing others.
- **Would love to** let go of the need to be in control, but doesn't trust life without having her hands on it or in it.

This book will focus on the first obstacle, **"Would love to make a change, but there's a fear of the unknown."** The other obstacles will be addressed in future books. In order to dispel the fear of the unknown and explore the manifold good things that can come from making a change and taking a leap of faith, I will begin by defining change, and then I will take you through some pivotal changes in my own life that helped build my character and self-esteem and brought me to the resolution to live a life of purpose on purpose.

Before I could embrace an abundant mindset and lifestyle, I had to truly believe that I had a God-given purpose. I had to face the negative script I was telling myself and replace it with a positive script. Only then could I accept and flow with the necessary changes that had to happen in my life.

You, too, have your own particular script, and I'll be providing you with keys along the way to recognize and understand it and space to work through it at the end of this book. Although I will not expound exegetically on the scriptures referenced throughout this book, each one is deeply significant to my spiritual journey. I pray that they will resonate with you as well.

No, my life's race isn't complete, but so far I've had to face all five of the aforementioned obstacles, and without embracing this first one, **change**, it would have been impossible for this book or www.tiffytalks.com to exist.

So if you're fed up with being fearful, of being afraid to let go of your old mindset, location, or vocation so that you can pursue the great work you're called to do, don't worry! In the pages ahead, you'll be strengthened to think about change in new ways—not as blah, but as a bridge—so you can embrace change and move forward in your calling. After you read this book, you will also be better equipped to see obstacles for what they are: as momentary delays that could become lifetime distractions, if allowed.

It's time to rethink change.

Are you ready to take this journey with me? Let's go.

With love,

P.S. I have to share with you, in the midst of working to complete this book, my years of studies and theological training finally bought me to my goal I'd been striving so long to complete: I was awarded my master's in divinity degree in May 2015. My gratitude is through the roof!!

CHAPTER ONE { RISKY BUSINESS

RISKY BUSINESS*

*{ **Change.** Why is it so scary? Why do many of us avoid change, although we know that it's a normal part of life?

The answer is pretty simple. Despite its normalcy, change at its core is risky business. By definition, risk includes the potential for loss; and loss, for many, brings about feelings of pain and anxiety.

But breathe easy, I'm not going to tell you that choosing to make a change is simple. It's actually a big deal, because movement towards change often triggers some degree of fear and pain. Even if the pain isn't real, the perception of pain is real. For instance, if you're being nudged to change your circle of friends, and you know it's for the best, your *mental cortex* begins to perceive life without them, which brings about feelings of anxiousness, remorse, or pain prior to the actual loss of friendships. So, in order to avoid the pain and possible drama, you might opt to hold onto the circle of friends and live with the discomforting comfort of remaining in their company.

I've been in this situation a time or few. Instead of following the internal nudge that said, "Move on!" I held on to people because the false impressions in my mind and the script I was telling myself persuaded me to imagine how horrible life would be without them.

Yes, the power of contemplating what was and what will no longer be can be a huge deterrent to making a needed change. But it's important to also note this: The *power of contemplating* various possibilities—a new and inspiring script of what could be—is a significant motivator as well, one that can positively open your mind to embrace and go after the change you desire most.

So, what is change?

Change is a shifting away from what was toward what will be—toward a new and different outcome. Unfortunately, it's the not knowing in advance what the different outcome will be that turns many people off from embracing change. It's important to emphasize that the fear associated with making a change or taking a leap of faith can be both external and internal. For instance, you could have a momentary external fear of moving to a new city, a warranted concern about having to get acclimated to a new place and new people, or you could be living daily with an internal fear of trusting people. This internal fear can be due to built-up anxiety based on your history with people, or it could stem from the environment you live in.

Whatever its cause, anxiety is an unfriendly culprit that fuels fear and makes you question your ability to make even the littlest of changes.

Typically, when confronted with change, the average person's mind begins to assess: *Okay, so what will I have to give up in order to change? Am I even capable of doing this? Who will I become in the process? And is it really worth it?*

Think about it.

The last time you contemplated a change, or if you're contemplating a change right now, did any of these questions come to mind? Do you know why they did? Why do you feel pressure when considering a life-changing decision? As you read parts of my story, you'll see that just thinking about what it takes to go from the old to the new can be overwhelming, which causes the most well-intentioned person to stick with what, whom, and where they are.

[1] Harriet Lerner, PhD, *Fear and Other Uninvited Guests* (New York: HarperCollins Publishers, 2004), 54.

> *"Anxiety tricks you into believing that you are lesser and smaller than you really are."* [1]
>
> ~Harriet Lerner, PhD

This is where the popular saying "Better the devil you know than the devil you don't know" comes to mind. The energy and maintenance it takes to live day in and day out with the familiar "devil," for lack of a better word, is rationalized in the mind as being easier and less painful than entertaining a new, unfamiliar devil. The painful reality is that one must be willing to make a sacrifice, a trade-off, a risky choice, despite the anxiety, fear, and illusions that invade the mind. In my experience, that's the only way to bury that known devil and go beyond it.

As Christie Cozad Neuger mentions in her book, Counseling Women, "Since many women place meaning and live our lives through the stories we have created,"[2] it's critical that the stories we tell ourselves, real or illusionary, are not in a passive voice, but in an active, enabling and empowering voice.

"For I am about to do something new. See, I have already begun! Do you not see it?"

~Isaiah 43:19

Until you and I can "see" the change, imagine a new story, and write a new script for our lives, the change that we desire the most will continue to evade us.

Key to consider:

WHAT SCRIPT DO YOU CURRENTLY REPLAY IN YOUR MIND ABOUT YOUR LIFE THAT YOU CAN'T IMAGINE LETTING GO OF?

[2] *Christie Cozad Neuger, Counseling Women (Minneapolis: Fortress Press, 2001), 86.*

CHAPTER TWO

{ # THE CHANGE YOU NEED IS SEEKING YOU

THE CHANGE YOU NEED IS SEEKING YOU*

It can be hard to see the change you need for yourself, but it's there trying to get your attention, seeking you out to introduce you to a new idea or a new person, working behind the scenes to point you toward the purpose you're designed to live. Maybe you're well aware that there is something going on in the atmosphere that's conspiring to call you to do more than you're ready for, so you're hesitant to answer the call and adamant to resist the changes that need to be made to get there.

But don't let me put words in your mouth.

* The change I needed was most certainly seeking me, but I was oblivious. I was heavily preoccupied with my life and how successful I thought I had to become in order to be accomplished and happy. Despite my aloofness and lack of awareness, however, I still received consistent and persistent divine signs throughout my life.

However, like a man in love with a woman, the Divine was determined to get my attention. Unbeknownst to me, I was being pursued and plotted on to become more aware of my purpose and myself and to really experience change and transformation on a major level for myself. I couldn't see the set-up back then, but now I know the change I needed most was seeking after me all of my life.

Truth is, had I not been sought after repeatedly by godly intervention to do something new and different with my life, I would have remained in the same city, the same relationship, and the same career—stuck in a good but unfulfilling rhythm of not being miserable yet not being happy and, more importantly, not being fulfilled.

"Jesus replied, 'You do not realize now what I am doing, but later you will understand"

~John 13:7

Key to consider:

WHAT VOCATIONAL THINGS WERE SPOKEN OVER YOU AS A CHILD, ADOLESCENT, OR ADULT? WERE YOU BEING TOLD YOU SHOULD SING, DANCE, WRITE, TEACH, ETC.? IS THERE A COMMON THREAD?

CHAPTER THREE

{ LEAVE MY MOUTH ALONE

LEAVE MY MOUTH ALONE*

My first memorable encounter with *change*, as it relates to my purpose, wasn't a good look or a good experience. It happened when I was an adolescent, in elementary or middle school, and I was being picked on because I had this ridiculously noticeable ring around my mouth.

Yep! I used to lick my lips.

As you can imagine, it was a tough habit to have as a tween. I can recall doing any and everything possible to keep my mouth covered up and to keep my lips off of everyone else's mouth. I think you get my point—being the subject of gossip never feels good, regardless of your age. Needless to say, I wasn't quick to smile or speak, because doing either would draw attention to me and to my mouth, and I didn't want that.

Nowadays, it's hard to keep me quiet, but back then, during that difficult time of life, speaking up was not as much fun as it is today.

Now, as I look back, the thought of it is both comical and sad, but it's significant to mention because now I can really see how my mouth—the main instrument that I needed to embrace in order to encourage and motivate others—was under attack at a very young age.

I'm convinced! We all run the risk of being made to feel insecure and naked in areas where we're the most gifted.

I know an incredible singer, who I coached in the areas of confidence and esteem and who was given a critical "wrong" opinion about her voice at a very young age. Because she respected the person who misjudged her gift, she took those harsh words as the truth about her vocal ability. More importantly, she allowed it to shape her script. The internal story echoing within her mind is "I can't sing!"

Is she singing today? Yes.

However, until she's able to set the record straight with herself and the world and rewrite the script about her crazy incredible gift of song, she will continue to sing with the negative script in mind, which will limit her ability to really—I mean really—s-i-n-g!

The security that comes with embracing and exercising our God-given gifts is more than enough to see us through, but sometimes it takes time to see that what we think is a weakness is in actuality a strength that has not been explored. That's why making a change for many of us is exactly what's needed in order to grasp all that is within us.

Although I eventually grew out of licking my lips, the shame I carried with me, and the insecurity that developed from habitually covering up my smile and my voice left a bruise of inadequacy within me. Undoubtedly, a negative change was imprinted in my self-esteem. I'm certain this was around the time when I began to dislike and devalue my face, my smile, and my voice.

I wish I had the courage back then to tell those kids to "Leave my mouth alone!"

Then again...

"You intended to harm me, but God intended it for good to accomplish what is now being done..."

~Genesis 50:20

Key to consider:

WHAT MIGHT YOU BE SHYING AWAY FROM, DENYING, OR DOUBTING ABOUT YOURSELF THAT COULD BE YOUR GREATEST GIFT TO OTHERS? MAYBE YOU'RE INSECURE IN AN AREA THAT GOD HAS ALREADY SECURED FOR YOU.

CHAPTER FOUR

AN UNINTENTIONAL BIRTH

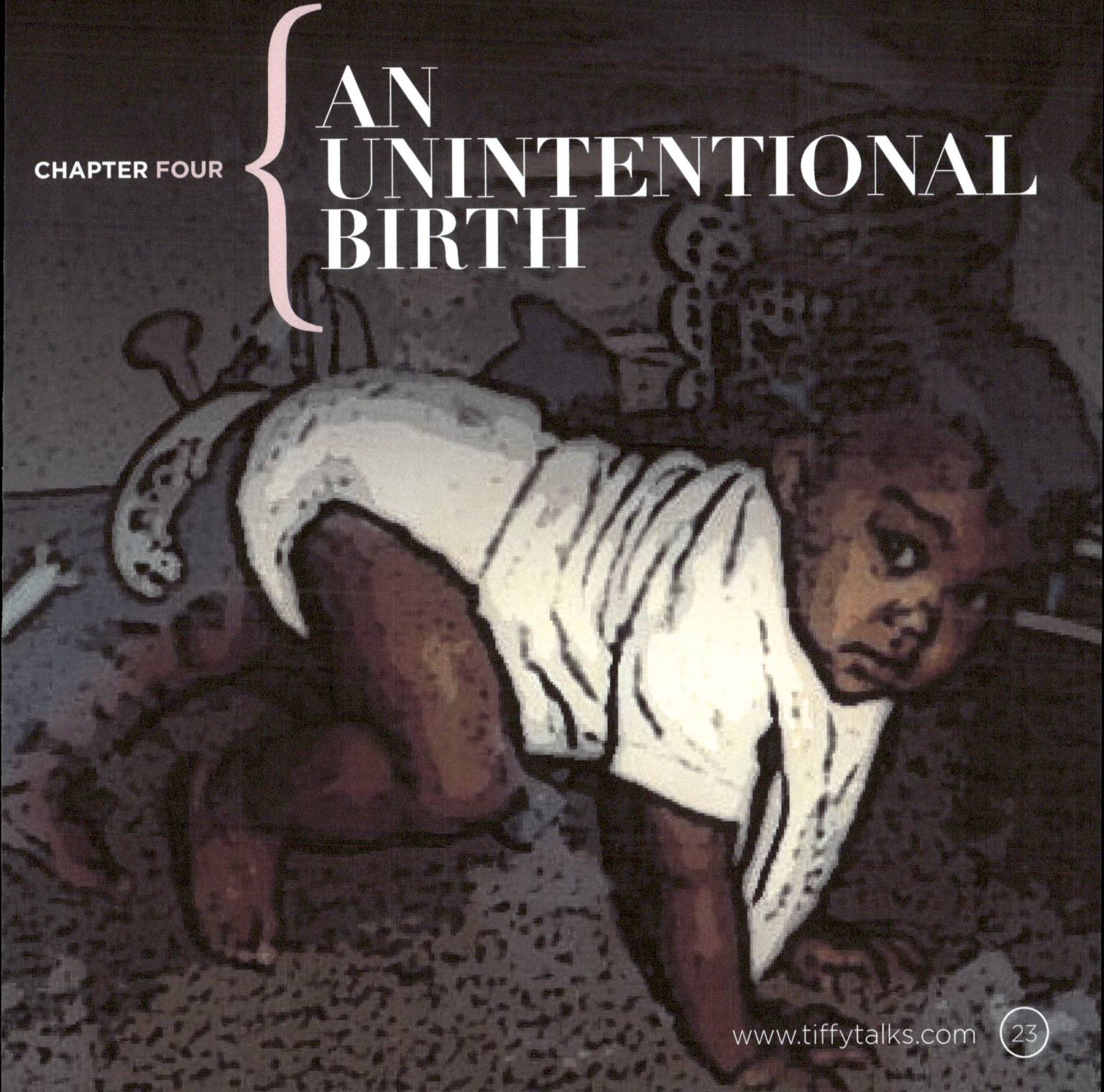

AN UNINTENTIONAL BIRTH*

As a teenager, I was cute, quirky, and smart, but I didn't know how cute I was, I totally resented my quirkiness, and I definitely didn't take my book smarts seriously. Instead of embracing my quirkiness and exercising my intelligence muscle, I was more consumed with the insecurities I had surrounding my overall looks and recuperating from the whole ring-around-the-mouth debacle.

Like many young girls, trying to fit in was important to me, and the bruise of inadequacy that formed in my adolescent years was starting to swell up inside me. It was starting to take a toll on my otherwise fun childhood. Since I had developed a warped perception about myself, the script in my head about my possibilities was limited, ugly, and tainted, which led me to make hasty and unhealthy choices, some choices that were unintentional but changed my life forever.

At the age of fifteen, one of my choices led to the birth of my daughter, Deja.

Being a teenager was short-lived for me. I went from hanging out at block parties to mixing Carnation® milk with iron drops. It was never my intention to have a child so young. I love my daughter, and she is by no means a mistake, but being a mom at fifteen was traumatic, and I didn't have a safe space to express how terrified I was to fail at it.

In the face of the weight and difficulty of my new role, instead of passing my daughter off on my mother (which she wasn't having anyway), I pushed past a lot of anxiety and fears and became overly determined and driven to live life on top. And by the world's standards, I did just that.

> *"If there is no struggle, there is no progress."* [1]
> ~*Frederick Douglass*

Eventually I defied every odd and every negative statistic for teenage moms. I worked harder than I knew I could to provide for us and to prove that I was more than the misguided decisions of my youth. Before I could blink, all the grinding, negotiating, and renegotiating I did in school, college, and at multiple workplaces was beginning to pay off. It took me longer than normal, but I completed my undergraduate degree and gladly welcomed every perk that came with my new achievement.

By the time I was in my early twenties, my life trajectory was showing signs of greatness, and so was my income level. I put my dependence on the system behind me, and although I don't promote teenage or unwed pregnancies, the unintentional birth of my daughter was actually the **change** I needed. Having to be responsible for her life set off a tremor in my faulty thinking and urged me to probe the question of my own significance.

But I was still fairly young, and I really wasn't ready to think so deeply and intentionally about myself just yet.

☞ *Key to consider:*

WHAT CHANGE HAVE YOU ALREADY GONE THROUGH THAT YOU THOUGHT YOU WOULDN'T MAKE IT THROUGH?

CHAPTER FIVE { # LIFE INTERRUPTED

LIFE INTERRUPTED*

*{ Based on my own experience and the experiences of many of the women I interviewed, sat in salons with, and know personally, I believe that one's choices and life experiences can set off shockwaves that aim to alert or awaken the individual to something she might be missing or needs to pay careful attention to. However, over time, due to an inability to get or receive the message, she could find herself in a full-throttle earthquake. *Remember, the change you need is seeking you.*

Let me explain.

By the time I reached my mid-twenties, life was really getting good. I was working for a cool firm, with cool people and cool perks. My daughter was in elementary school, and I was bubbly in love with my beau-friend. I was sitting on the tippy top of my "A" game, with my feet dangling and arms waving. While I was enjoying being on top, without my knowledge and far beyond what my eyes could see there were some critical shockwaves routed to rock the core of my life, to ***change*** me in ways that I could have never predicted.

Since things had been going so well for me, personally and professionally, I never stopped to consider, "What if this life that I was so determined and driven to create doesn't work out?" At that point in my life, I was certainly naïve and not in tune with the fact that all my efforts to be in control and all my well-meaning tactics to be successful didn't necessarily mean bad things wouldn't happen to me.

I had to learn the hard way.

Despite how smart and successful I was, I couldn't prevent bad things or **change** from happening. Within three years, a major category 7 earthquake hit me, and my world was never the same.

Looking to upgrade, I left my cool job for a cooler .com job, and within several months I got laid off. The loss of my job sent jolts through my identity and cushy lifestyle. I was devastated. Like, excuse me, I liked traveling to top cities and staying in the best hotels. I liked going to professional mixers and touting my sales credentials. I also liked those paychecks and zipping around town like money wasn't a thing. Being laid off was not in the plans. I was in a very vulnerable place, but I didn't want anyone to know that I was sweating a mac 9 with bullets inside. I was so scared to lose everything I worked so hard to achieve. I wasn't ready to give up the "she's on her 'A' game" script.

> *"Change requires a breaking down before there's a building up."*
>
> ~Nancy Duarte, resonate

Being forced to **change** can be the worst. It can feel like a death, and major resentment can build up within you, as well as bouts with grief. "In times of loss, spiritual beliefs can provide solace but also can be a source of confusion when life events contradict these beliefs."[3] Since I had no understanding of spiritual matters at that time in my life, my mind resorted to a lot of questioning and comparing myself to others: "Why me and not her?" "How could this happen?" I had to learn that sometimes it's so critical that we get to the next place that is intended for us that an unwanted change or interruption has to take place in order to push us toward it.

⚷ Key to consider:

WHAT HAVE YOU LOST THAT MAY BE NEGATIVELY IMPACTING THE WAY YOU SEE YOURSELF AND YOUR FUTURE?

[3] Mary Thomas Burke, Jane C. Chauvin & Judith G. Miranti, *Religious and Spiritual Issues in Counseling* (Brunner-Routledge: New York, 2005), 135.

CHAPTER SIX

{ CHANGE HURTS BUT HELPS

CHANGE HURTS BUT HELPS*

I was in the midst of a life-changing, life-threatening, emotional, physical and spiritual earthquake that I naively thought could be resolved by getting a fancier and more financially stable job. It wasn't that simple. See, the loss of my job now provided me with this window of opportunity to stop and look at my life. A couple of pages back, I said to you, "I wasn't really ready to think so deeply and intentionally about myself just yet."

Well, the time had come.

Now I was being gifted with the time to face the reality of my life—the good, the bad, and the funky. And after the major breach that happened with the loss of my job, I couldn't help but notice all these other cracks—gaps that had been there all along in my life and my relationships, gaps that were neglected or overlooked but could no longer be ignored.

Do you ever think to yourself, "Something's not right in this situation," but you don't know what, or maybe you're too afraid to put your finger on it? It's like you can smell deception or dis-ease in the air, whether it's coming from those you love or from within yourself. Maybe you can sense what the problem is, and you know it has to be addressed or changed, but you don't have the energy or heart to lay the cards on the table.

Truth is, my relationship was fizzling, and my daughter was starting to rebel against my authority. The things I cared about the most were beginning to unravel. I was in over my head, and had been for most of my life, yet I didn't know to change or what exactly needed to be changed. I know I didn't want to experience any more loss or pain. I wanted to hold on to the sameness of what I had, because it was comfortable. I couldn't picture anything different, and I didn't have a backup script. Plus, I couldn't admit to myself or anyone else that my plans were beginning to crumble.

I was confused, disappointed, and hurt. My thoughts were scattered and piling up on me: "What am I going to do now? Is my relationship over? How could my daughter be so rebellious? Couldn't she see how hard I was working?"

I had no idea that one change, losing my job, would impact other key areas of my life so much. Have you ever stubbed your toe and shut down for a few minutes until the pain goes away? Like, look, give me a minute! That's how I felt, but the pain I was feeling didn't go away in a few minutes. I was so emotional and so fearful of what was next. Mysteriously, though, behind the scenes, the anguish I was experiencing was going to be used to help me.

Yes, to help me.

See, for the first time ever, I was starting to lose faith in my plans and starting to wonder if there was a larger plan for my life, a purpose that was bigger than anything I could create on my own.

Key to consider:

WHAT'S THE GREATEST, GRANDEST PLAN (DREAM) THAT YOU HAVE FOR YOUR LIFE?

"For I know the plans I have for you," declares the Lord, "plans to prosper you and not to harm you, plans to give you hope and a future."

~Jeremiah 29:11

CHAPTER SEVEN { CHANGE IS A CHOICE

CHANGE IS A CHOICE*

My motivation for being a top achiever was dwindling, and I was running out of bright ideas and strategic plans. Despite my solid sales background, I was having a tough time finding a fancier and more financially secure job. Eventually I begrudgingly interviewed with a top consumer products company. I wasn't in love with the brand or the position, but the people and perks were nice. Plus, after several months of being without work, I was ready to reclaim my former lifestyle.

*{ Finally, I was offered a decent position, but there was a catch. This time I had to choose to make a significant **change**, on top of all the other changes that were going on in my life.

I had to relocate?!?

If you're anything like me, and you can't quite picture life without having family and friends around, then you know that the offer to relocate was way beyond foreign. I was like, "So let me process this. You want me to leave the only area I know and the people I love—for what? Seclusion?"

Nuts!!!

Seriously, for me, relocating was like asking me to give up my parental rights. I was so attached to my family and my budding social life. Remember, I'm still in my twenties with a child and a beau-friend. Needless to say, I was petrified to leave my hometown. I had a lot to think about in a short amount of time. *Okay, so I wasn't pleased with my overall lot in life, but moving was a dramatic way to deal with my gripes.*

I was conflicted. On the one hand, I knew I didn't have to accept the job, but on the other hand, I had this airy feeling that this was my big chance, although for what I had no idea.

Needless to say, the deliberation process was dramatic and heartfelt, but at the same time it was weird. I didn't call my parents for advice, and I didn't have a mentor at the time to hash things over with, but I do recall pressing my beau-friend for guidance. (Laugh with me.) What did he do? He held his tongue and essentially refrained from deciding for me. Instead he insisted I do what I wanted to do, even if it meant I'd be leaving our relationship behind.

So, I had to make the choice, and I did.

At one of the most tumultuous times in American history, weeks after the Twin Towers were attacked in New York City, I shocked my loved ones and myself. I chose to leave EVERYTHING I loved behind, except my daughter, for something new and different.

"Leave your native country, your relatives, and your father's family, and go to the land that I will show you."

~Genesis 12:1

Key to consider:

WHAT RISK WOULD YOU TAKE IF AGE, MONEY, OR THE OPINIONS OF OTHERS DIDN'T MATTER?

CHAPTER **EIGHT** {

BUT HEALTHY

CHANGE IS SCARY BUT HEALTHY*

In my late twenties, when I took the leap of faith to leave my family and friends, to relocate to a foreign land, I didn't have any spiritual awareness or prayer life. However, I did have this heavy sense that if I continued to hold on to the sameness of what was comfortable and familiar, I would miss a great opportunity to explore new and different outcomes for my life.

Despite the fear I felt, I knew that I had to go out in the world to become more than I ever imagined for myself.

"I've found you're better able to love once you have embodied love from within."
~@tiffytalks

It was the scariest, yet healthiest decision I could have made. It was out in the strange land of Pennsylvania (smile with me) that I accepted God's love, and I slowly was led to engage myself and the world in ways that I had never done before. It's hard to explain, but in all the chasing I did of men, corporate ladders, even friends, I was missing out on being truly engaged with myself—the good, the bad, and the funky sides of me.

It's truly incredible, the change that was seeking me all of my life, eventually caught up to me, and has manifested itself in extraordinary ways, but I had to keep going in the face of the scariest twists and turns of my life.

You may find yourself in a scary, peculiar place. Maybe you're at a crossroads, unsure of which direction to take, or maybe you know you're being called to change your current position or posture in life. Before you go any further, it's important that you realize that you are not alone in your questioning. There are a lot of other women out there who are very concerned about what's next and what's best. Here's what some of the women I interviewed had to say:

"Am I enough for life, for God"

~N. Miller, 46

"I fear being alone."

~Alicia, 30

"Without knowing my purpose, I fear I will be in a state of perpetual discontent."

~N. Strong, 34

"Will I get married?"

~Tiffany, 25

"Why am I so confused?"

~Chassity, 29

Thoughts like these can haunt the soul, but they don't have to. In order to go beyond a place of frustration and questioning, to get to a place of satisfaction and resolve, it's important to embrace change as a means to introducing you to new and different options you may not otherwise have considered. You also must work to replace whatever negative connotations you have of change with some positive associations.

Key to consider:

WHAT SCARES YOU THE MOST?

CHAPTER NINE

{ IT'S TIME TO RETHINK CHANGE

IT'S TIME TO RETHINK CHANGE*
THINK BUTTERFLIES!

The butterfly can't choose its metamorphosis, but people can.

A butterfly has to go through a divinely orchestrated process of four stages of growth in order to become all that it is, and each stage serves a vital purpose for the butterfly to survive and thrive. Butterflies, unlike humans, have no choice but to change and change and change again, and at the end of their metamorphosis, the "fullness" of life for the butterfly is manifested.

*{ Fortunately people are not confined to a set metamorphic process to become all that we're meant to be and do. Each of us has a unique path toward becoming authentically and fully human, and, though our paths are divinely influenced, our cooperation and engagement are required if we are to go beyond striving to thriving. Therefore, unlike the butterfly, you and I must choose to be transformed, to make a change, and another change and another change if we are to live a fully manifested life.

This gives us some exciting incentive to get involved in our growth process and to hopefully think of change as just one of the many ways in which God can steer us closer and closer to the connections, encounters, and experiences that are meant for us.

Key to consider:
WHAT CAN YOU LEARN FROM THE BUTTERFLY'S METAMORPHOSIS?

IT'S TIME TO RETHINK CHANGE*
THINK BRIDGE NOT BLAH!

If you have apprehension, concern, or fear of change, try not to picture change as a dark abyss of nothingness, but more like a bridge. With most bridges, you can't quite see all there is on the other side, but nonetheless it's worth traveling over to encounter and explore what's waiting there.

See, on the other side of change are people, places, and positions that would be inaccessible to you if you erred on the side of sameness. There's an unfortunate misconception that holding onto sameness is the safe and secure option and that change should be cautioned against, but in plenty of situations remaining in the same place is detrimental and makes a fully manifested life impossible.

*{ You may know a woman who's afraid to let go of the safety net of an unhealthy relationship or an unfulfilling job. There was a time when I was crippled by fear, constantly worried about what I would lose—so much so that I barely considered what I would gain if I loosened my grip and opened myself up to a new possibility.

Due to shortsightedness, many of us struggle against going beyond what we believe, what we know, or what we see. Whether we're willing to admit it or not, the courage and faith it requires to go bigger, bolder, or broader is difficult at best, but mysteriously I've found that God uses bridges of change to help us gain more clarity and confidence ... if we're willing to take the steps.

⚬—Key to consider:
WHAT WOULD YOU GAIN IF YOU MOVED IN A NEW DIRECTION OR MOVED TOWARD THE CHANGE YOU'RE BEING CALLED TO MAKE?

IT'S TIME TO RETHINK CHANGE*
THINK COMPLETE BLISS!

The right change at the right time could lead to exceptional moments of complete bliss.

How cliché does this sound, "You deserve the best and nothing less?!" You may have seen this quote floating around social media, or maybe a good friend said this to you in order to encourage you. (Wink with me.) Despite, the commonness of this saying, I do believe there's such a thing as divine alignment with what and who is best, and when the alignments happen, at the right time and with the right people, you'll know. It will be hard to explain, or, depending on your personality, no explanation will be necessary, because you'll be perfectly at peace with knowing that what you've found or encountered is blissful.

"Be still, and know that I am God..."

~Psalm 46:10

Sometimes, it's not something super-deep. It could happen when you're out taking a walk and you bump into a stranger and end up having an amazing conversation, or instead of ignoring the blue jay that just flew by, you actually stop and experience what is happening around you. You slow down enough to take in what's really going on in your midst.

I've found bliss in the stillness of life. God slowed me down so I could value my beauty, the beauty in others, and the beauty in nature.

True story: On two occasions, I was showered by ladybugs. (*Say "What?" with me.*) The first time, I was standing on a porch in South Carolina, and ladybugs began to fall on me, one by one, on my head, shoulders, and arms. On the other occasion, while I was sitting in my parked car in Philadelphia, ladybug after ladybug kept flying into my windshield.

It didn't take long for me to see that something special was happening. It was hard to explain, but I knew that the ladybugs were a miraculously positive sign. Each time, I felt a breeze of contentment and love in the air. It may sound silly, but the ladybug showers encouraged me to persevere and fight for my purpose, despite how much I wanted to give up. It was like God was winking at me, and instead of discounting the experiences as random, I held them close as divine.

See, **change** isn't just about physically moving toward a new or different outcome. It's also about being mentally and spiritually open enough to allow in a new way of thinking and a new way of relating to the world around us. When we do this, we increase our ability to experience moments of complete bliss.

Key to consider:

DOES CONSIDERING CHANGE AS AN OPPORTUNITY TO EXPERIENCE MORE BLISS IN YOUR LIFE MAKE YOU UNCOMFORTABLE? IF SO, WHY?

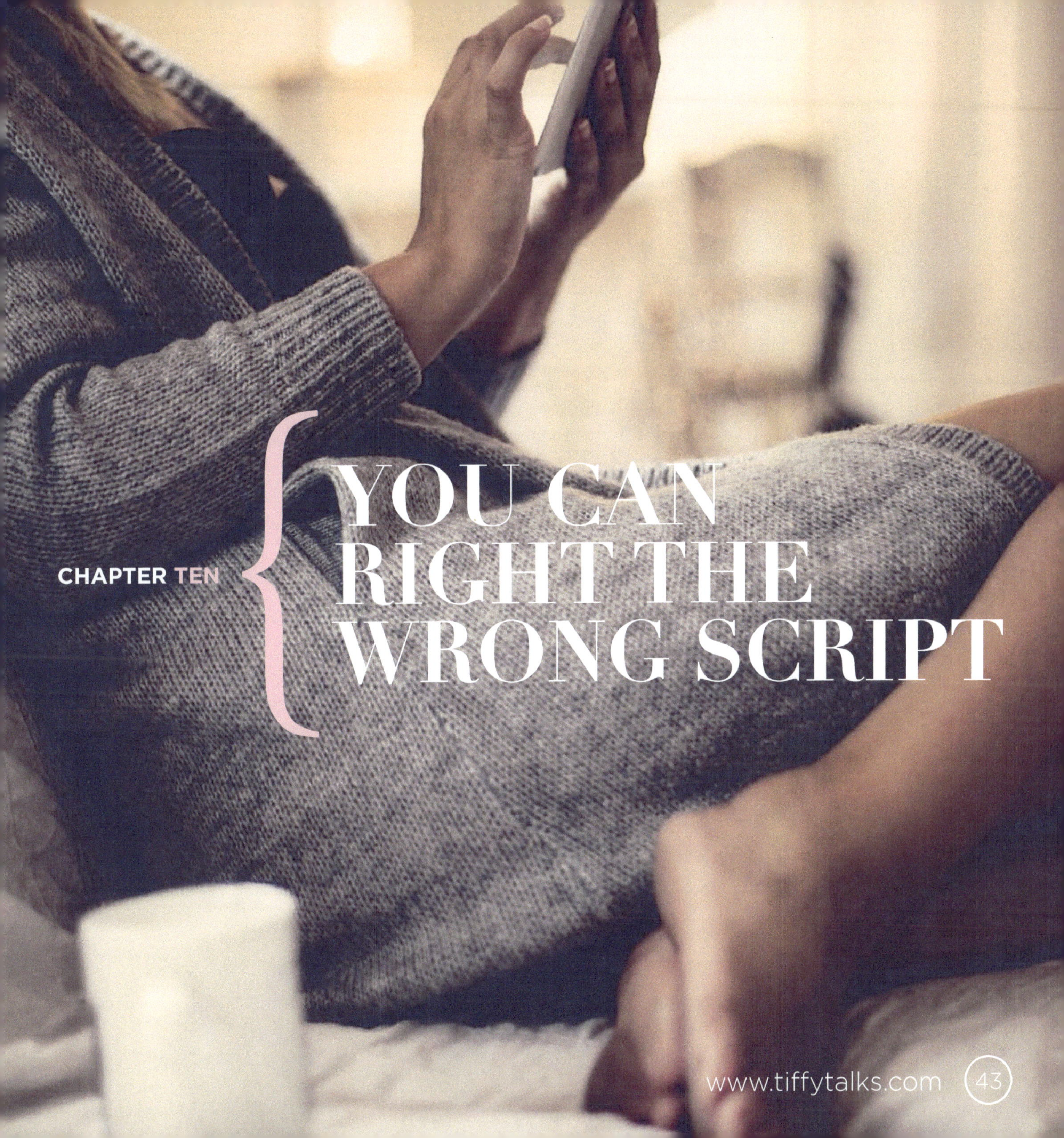

CHAPTER TEN

YOU CAN RIGHT THE WRONG SCRIPT

YOU CAN RIGHT THE WRONG SCRIPT*

{ The keys to consider throughout this book were designed to help you gain clarity about any apprehension or fear you have about change and to help you expand your view of change, so change or having to make a change will no longer be an obstacle, but a welcomed opening towards a fully manifested life.

If you weren't able to work through the questions as you read along, here's a list of the keys to consider again.

1. What old script do you keep replaying in your mind about you or your life that's been hard to let go?

2. What vocational things were spoken over you as a child, adolescent, or adult, i.e., that you should sing, dance, write, teach, etc.? Is there a common thread?

3. What might you be shying away from, denying or doubting about yourself that could be your greatest gift to others? Maybe you're insecure in an area that God has already secured for you.

4. What change have you already gone through that you thought you wouldn't make it through?

5. What have you lost that may be negatively impacting the way you see yourself and your future?

6. What's the greatest, grandest plan (dream) that you have for your life?

7. What risk would you take if age, money, or the opinions of others didn't matter?

8. What scares you the most?

9. What can you learn from the butterfly's metamorphosis?

10. What would you gain if you moved in a new direction or moved toward the change you're being called to make?

11. Does considering change as an opportunity to experience more bliss in your life make you uncomfortable? If so, why?

12. Bonus Key to Consider: What intangible and tangible assets are you confident you possess personally and professionally, right now? For example, intangible assets are you're naturally personable and spiritually aware, tangible assets are you have 5 years of sales experience and you speak Spanish. List them below.

_____

_____

_____

_____

_____

_____

_____

_____

_____

Now that you've answered the keys to consider and you've been presented with some new ways to think about change, take some time to reflect on the old script that's been preventing you from unlocking the life and love you desire. Can you hear the old script ringing in your ears? Write down that old script (you're going to release) here.

_____

_____

_____

_____

When you're ready, it's important for you to confidently replace the old prohibitive script with a new affirming script. Here's a true personal example: My old script, "Why did I have to move away from my family?" Which kept my mindset in a sad and lonely place. My new script, "I had to move away from my hometown in order to grow into the woman I've become today." Which inspires my mindset, in a "you go girl" kind of way for taking the leap of faith. Okay, it's your turn. You can right the wrong script, do it here.

_____

_____

_____

_____

I'm seriously excited for you! The key questions to consider were designed to help you see how much the life and love you desire is already divinely planted inside of you. It just takes some digging to get to all that gold. Let this new script lead you toward the change you desire most, and when you're tempted to digress or give up, meditate on the truth and possibilities in your new story, your new amazing script.

SHARE THIS BOOK WITH OTHERS*

*{ Well, you –we did it! You took the journey with me through the first #GetEngaged book, Volume 1 is done. *If you enjoyed this book and got a gem out of it, please share it with others.*

Here's how...

Share via your social media networks and tag me:
LinkedIn: www.linkedin.com/in/tiffytalks
Facebook: TiffyTalks
Instagram: @tiffytalks
Periscope: @tiffytalks
Twitter: @_tiffytalks

ABOUT
THE AUTHOR

Tiffany Wilson is an author, founder of www.tiffytalks.com, life coach to millennial women and an inspirational speaker. She holds a Master of Divinity degree and has a gift of empowering women to let go of their fears, step out in faith and #GetEngaged with their lives.

Tiffany knows first-hand what it's like to get knocked down by life. She has experienced living with a severe loss of self-confidence and self-love, as well as living life not knowing who she was or the direction she was going. Through the grace of God and guidance from others, Tiffany was awakened to her mental, physical and spiritual power.

Tiffany birthed www.tiffytalks.com, a powerful platform to share what she has learned through her experiences and offer wisdom on topics related to love, relationships and faith.

For three years, Tiffany led the "TwentySomethings" by Christian Talk Therapy, a group-coaching program that helped young women overcome life's challenges and integrate godly principles into their daily lives. She has spoken at various conferences and facilitated workshops on "self-esteem", "self-worth", and "self-love."

Tiffany's practical coaching and spirited speaking style guides women in resolving life's questions such as, "am I enough, who am I" and "what is my purpose in the world"? If you're ready to get more engaged with you and your purpose, go to www.tiffytalks.com and download the free Busy Woman's Cheat Sheet to Staying Spiritually Strong.

THANKS FOR SHARING YOUR GIFTS AND TALENTS WITH ME.*

{
* {
Jeff Fuller, *Graphic Designer*
Leslie Komarnicki, *Editor*
Dr. Mayra Picos-Lee, *Professor*
Jamila Payne, *Entrepreneurship Trainer*
Min. Jennell L. Williams, *Spiritual Sister*

ADDITIONAL RESOURCES

Johnson, Kenneth, M.D. and Kenneth Blanchard. *Who Moved My Cheese?* New York: G.P. Putnam's Sons, 2000.

Lerner, Harriet, Ph.D. *Fear and Other Uninvited Guests.* New York: HarperCollins Publishers, 2004.

Paulus, Trina. *Hope for the Flowers.* Charlotte, NC: Newman Press, 1972.

PHOTO CREDITS*

*{
1. Pg. 14, Brooklyn Bridge with the Rain, New York City by Gagliardi Photography via Canva.com

2. Pg. 18, Pink Field, https://www.flickr.com/photos/4629178484

3. Pg. 21, Tiffany Screaming by www.whitneythomas.com

4. Pg. 24, Deja Having Fun, Personal Picture

5. Pg. 27, Jenny Downing, Pigeon Toes, https://www.flickr.com/photos/rocketboom/4475361568

6. Pg. 30, Moody Image of Woman Looking Down by Unsplash via Canva.com

7. Pg. 33, Parker Knight, Reception – 0249, https://www.flickr.com/photos/jenny-pics/8109837536

8. Pg. 36, Mathias Miranda, Eterea (Girl Sunset) https://www.flickr.com/photos/mathiasmiranda/12162075654/

9. Pg. 39, A Close Up Shot of a Paper Kite Butterfly (Idea leuco noe) by macro pixel via Canva.com

10. Pg. 43, Flying Lady Bug Insect by Lineartestpilot via Canva.com

11. Pg. 44, Woman on Couch, Istock 000046977650

12. Pg. 49, Taylor Hendrixson

www.ingramcontent.com/pod-product-compliance
Lightning Source LLC
LaVergne TN
LVHW072112070426
835509LV00003B/120